4 Solid Building Blocks to Fulfilling Your Dreams:
Unlocking the Greatness within You

Jenks Brutus

Copyright 2018 *Jenks Brutus*. **All rights reserved. No part of this book can be reproduced in any form without the written permission of the author and its publisher.**

Table of Contents

Acknowledgements 4
Foreword 6
My Story and I'm Sticking to It 8
Danger! Danger! Danger! 19
Decide To Take Full Responsibility for Your Life 23
Building Block # 1 37
Building Block # 2 49
Building Block # 3 62
Building Block # 4 76
The Purpose Decision Test 84
Author's Page 88

Acknowledgements

I would like to thank an all loving God who has a plan for all of our lives. Plans to prosper you, and not to harm you, plans to give you hope and a future. I would also like to thank my beautiful wife Nancy for always having my back. Thank you Precious for being my lover, friend, and most of all my partner on this journey called life. I would also like to thank my children Joshua, Jacob, Justice, Jurnee, Jedidiah, Hannah, and Sarah. To my Dad (See you in the resurrection), Mom, Brothers and their Wives, you guys are my "WHY". To Influence Team Difference Makers, John Maxwell, Les Brown, Jack Canfield, Craig Valentine and World Class Speakers, Lisa Nichols Speak and Write Community,

KIDD Marketing, Best Sellers Guild community, and all of you who have been put on my path, on this journey, this moment would not have been a reality without you. Your encouragements, words of comfort, your belief in me, your motivation, taking the time to pour into me your wisdom, your faith, is why we are celebrating today.

"It is amazing what you can accomplish if you do not care who gets the credit."

Harry S Truman.

"Talent wins games, but teamwork and intelligence win championships."

Michael Jordan

Today I celebrate *Your* win. Today I celebrate *Your* victory. Today *You* are the real champions. *We* did it!

Foreword

If you've been looking for a great book that keeps it 100% real with you but more importantly pushes you to keep it 100% real with yourself, then look no further. In this book, my good friend Jenks breaks down four building blocks that can completely transform your way of thinking and your way of life. His passion is to see you win and his mission is to make sure you do.

Not only does he lay out a blue print for you to follow but he also gives you the resources and tools to begin building your dream life immediately. There are many reasons why people stay stuck in life. Through his own personal experiences and training, Jenks has been able to provide you with principals that will help give you clarity on how to get to where you want to go, more quickly.

Throughout this book you will find several thought provoking questions that you must answer in order to get unstuck and continue building. After reading this book I am confident that you will find yourself taking massive action in building the life you've always dreamed of. As Jenks has mentioned in this book, "Now is the time," to start taking control of your future.

Jenks, I am so proud of you! Keep on making an impact and shaking the world!

Jose Flores

Mental Toughness Expert, International Motivational Speaker, and Author of, "Don't Let Your Struggle Become Your Standard."

My Story and I'm Sticking to It

Billionaire oil tycoon H.L. Hunt was once asked, "What was the secret of success?" He replied that for one to be successful he had to do only three things. First, one must know exactly what it is they want. Second, one must determine the price they're willing to pay to get what they want, and third, which involves action, get busy paying the price for what you want. I am a firm believer that for one to succeed at anything there can be no gap in between in following these steps. These success principles have been the hallmark, along with God's blessings for where I am today. I have the freedom in devoting my life to helping others achieve their dreams and spend more quality time with my family. I have the privilege of seeing my kids come home from school and spend time with them in helping them with their homework. I have been fortunate to travel to Africa, the Philippines, the Dominican Republic, and various places here in the United States inspiring others with the hope that life is worth living in their purpose. While all of these accolades are amazing I must humbly tell you that it wasn't always like this for me. A chronic procrastinator, living life as a wandering generality, a lot of ideas, but no direction in accomplishing them. A good talker, but no action, and an exceedingly fear of success. I was doing well in my vocation but feeling like a small boat without a sail. One of the lowest points of my life was when my wife of eight years and I got a divorce. I often tell my friends I wouldn't wish this experience on my worst enemy. The feelings of emotions that often comes along with divorce began to take a huge toll on me. I remember driving home from work one sunny day, as I had on other days, when all of a sudden, I began to experience a panic attack. Because this was the first time I was experiencing this type of emotion I literally thought I was going to die. I do not know if you have ever had a panic attack before, but it feels like your heart is racing to jump out of your chest. It literally felt like somebody was holding my head under water and I was struggling to breathe. I began to experience shortness of breath, and the left side of my body began to tingle from my head all the way down to my feet. Today I can laugh about this, but I remember saying to myself, "God please don't let me die today" "I want to live" "I want to live". There were days I couldn't sleep through the night, and I literally thought that my life was over. I started losing weight, I was depressed all the time, and literally thought I was beginning to lose my mind. I felt as if the rug had been pulled right from underneath my foot, and I couldn't do anything about it. I had already doubted myself, but this divorce only increased what I had already believed about myself to be true. I remember thinking out loud "what a failure am I". During this season of darkness, I allowed my circumstances to affect everything I put my hands into sabotaging everything before I even began. I couldn't keep a job let alone stay focus on one thing to get done. One night I was beginning to have a panic and found my way to the emergency room, what would be many trips to the emergency room, only to be asked by the nurse, "Do I need to admit you upstairs?" Upstairs meaning the mental ward unit. What happened to be one of the worst moments of my life, ended up in disguise, being one of the best teaching moments of my life. It was at this moment, in my darkest hour, a friend of mine said to me "You have no one to blame but yourself for why you find yourself in this situation. At first, I thought that my friend was crazy, but reflecting on what was said I came to the realization at that moment that I had been blaming everyone else but me for why I was in the situation I was in. I blamed others for why I had not succeeded, and I blamed my ex-wife for why my life was miserable. When my friend said to me I am responsible it made me take one hard look at myself. Fast forward into the future I went and brought a book by Jack Canfield entitled "The Success Principle". To be honest at that time I did not read the entire book except the first chapter entitled, "Take 100% Responsibility for your Life". `That chapter thought me that the reason many do not succeed is that they will not take responsibility for where they are in their life right now. From reading that first chapter I discovered that I had all along been blaming my circumstances for where I was in my life and did not understand that it was my response to the circumstances that was giving me the results I had. For the first time in my life I began taking responsibility for the decisions I had made. Owning up to why I was where I was, and why I was divorced. From that point on my focused changed and I decided I may not be able to control the events, but I can control how I respond to them. I began to incorporate the four principles I will later spell out in detail in this book, and my life since is no longer dwelling in the graveyard of despair. I want you to understand that when I started to take 100% responsibility for where I was most of my symptoms, the panic attracts, the worrying, self-doubting all dissipated. Today I have been privileged to have impacted the lives of thousands of people giving them the hope that no matter how bad their lives may be right now there is always hope. This experience has created a passion in me to share with you the message of incorporating these four-success principles in your life in order to accomplish your dreams. I'm sharing these principles with you because if these core principles become the hallmark of your life you will go from procrastinator to action taker. This book is my commitment in aiding you in the effort of helping you to live your life to the fullest by achieving your dreams and helping others live their dreams along your journey. A friend and author of the book "6 degrees" took these steps in writing her first book with a very hectic schedule. A single mom of two beautiful girls, a full-time student studying to become a Forensic Scientist, and yes now an author. How did she do it? She knew what she wanted to do. She was willing to pay the price, and lastly, she put a plan of action together. I believe that these steps, if put into practice, can help you to accomplish anything. My beautiful wife,

Nancy, of Haitian descent, who is a nurse, and my hero, put these steps into operation to accomplish her dream of becoming a nurse. Without the financial support of her family put herself through school full-time while at the same time working full-time. Till this day I still don't know how she did it. If you were to sit down and talk to her she would tell you that she had a burning desire to become a nurse. That desire translated into a determination to pay the price even losing sleep many a night, and a plan of action to accomplish what she wanted. One of the greatest inspirational speakers of our time Zig Ziglar says, *"The elevator to success is out of order, but the stairs are always open."* On those stairs was the decision to climb them, a decision to pay the price, a plan of action to get to the top.

Brian Tracy, the Author of No Excuses! The Power of Self-Discipline says, *"Here's the rule: "If you do what other successful people do, repeatedly, nothing can stop you from eventually enjoying the same rewards that they do. But if you don't do what successful people do, nothing can help you."* Successful people from all walks of life follow these principles. This book, although a short one, will help you become a treasure to your soul if you are willing to follow the steps we will explore together in this book. This book is for you if you feel your life is at a standstill. If you are at a point in your life where you are tired of living by everyone else's set of rules. If you are ready to take control of your life, then you are in the right place. You will pick up tools to inspire you from the feeling of being stuck to implementing key strategic tools in reaching your goals. In this book you will find a blueprint that many have followed to achieve their dreams. You will find a blueprint that if you put it into practice will give you the time to do the things you want to, time for your family, and the freedom to live every day in your purpose. So, sit back, relax, and let us go on this journey together.

Danger! Danger! Danger!

Not following or living in your purpose is like taking a left turn when your GPS system says take a right turn.

You may be reading this and all kinds of fears maybe trying to talk yourself out of living in your purpose. The inner voices of self-doubt, pessimism, and "what ifs" maybe trying to keep you from moving forward on the path of living in your purpose. I understand your fears. Not implementing these four building blocks had kept me in constant fear in basking in my own set of circumstances, living according to everyone else's set of rules, and living to try and please everyone. I was constantly stressed out, and this led to a life of stress, lack of focus, and lack of drive. You see I had great ideas, but I did not have clarity. Ideas, but no game plan. Ideas, but no will to take action. Not implementing these four building blocks delayed my journey of living life to my fullest possibilities. It kept me a prisoner in my own skin. If only I had done this sooner in implementing these four principles I would be so much further than I am today. I wasted so much time worrying about what others might think. Sometime ago a friend of mine and I had a burden to begin a non-profit organization in a certain part of town where we lived. We wanted to help people by providing life skill classes, educational resources, aiding families with their teens in implementing programs to keep them off the streets and into the mind frame of going to college. By not implementing these four building blocks our focus shifted to all the negative backlash we got from well-meaning individuals who thought they were only looking out for our best of interest. Does that sound familiar? My friend and I missed out on a great opportunity to add value by serving a community that really needed it at the time. These building blocks are the same tools that numerous men and women have utilized to fulfill their dream. You might be asking how can these four building blocks really help? They can help you like it did for me. They will serve you as a vehicle to help you go from being stuck to being action oriented. A vehicle to go from having a lack of focus to being focus. These building blocks will get you out of that mindset where you feel you have no control over your life to now living a life with meaning and with purpose.

These four building blocks will give birth to that dream that has been hibernating in you, waiting to be born.

Decide To Take Full Responsibility for Your Life

"The greatest day in your life and mine is when we take total responsibility for our attitudes. That's the day we truly grow up."
John Maxwell

Have you ever awakened early in the morning before your household was awake? You could hear the quiet hush still the quietness of the moment as you are the only one to witness its majestic silence. It was to this scene I had awakened one morning to spend some personal time with God. This is a daily practice I have kept for years. After my personal time, I said to my lovely wife who happened to be sitting on the bed with me that morning, "Precious, I'm afraid that the end of the year is going to come, and as I have done every year, I would come to the realization that I accomplish nothing significant enough worth talking about. Have you ever felt that way? You see it was now April of 2016 and the year seemed to be flying by. I said to myself what have I done that is worth talking about so far, this year? You see in time past I would go through the year, complete some things but never anything I would deem significant enough to talk about. I would try and wing it without setting any concrete goals. I would come up with excuse after excuse, blaming everyone else for why I had I not achieve what I wanted to achieve. I have learned that if you are going to be successful before you endeavor to decide what you want you must first decide to take 100% responsibility for where you are in your life right now. A life well lived is fueled by taking personal responsibilities. Jack Canfield in his book, "The Success Principles" says, *"If you want to be successful, you have to take 100% responsibility for everything that you experience in your life. This includes the level of your achievements, the results you produce, the quality of your relationships, the state of your health and physical fitness, your income, your debts, your feelings—everything!"* Have you taken responsibility for your life for where you are right now? Or are you in the habit, as I was, of blaming everyone else. In that same book, Jack Canfield tells a personal story about an experience he had with W. Clement Stone back in 1969, one year short of my existence. W. Clement Stone, a self-made multimillionaire worth $600 million asked Jack Canfield a question that changed his life. W. Clement Stone asked, "If he took 100% responsibility for his life?" Jack replied by saying, "I think so" Wanting a more definite answer W. Clement Stone said, "This is a yes or no question, young man. You either do or you don't." Jack, stunned by the straight forwardness of Mr. Stone could only reply by saying, "Well I guess I'm not sure." Mr. Clement Stone went on say to the young Canfield, *"Taking one hundred percent responsibility means you acknowledge that you create everything that happens to you. It means you understand that you are the cause of all of your experience. If you want to be really successful, and I know you do, then you will have to give up blaming and complaining and take total responsibility for your life"*. Have you taken one hundred percent responsibility for your life. Have you stop blaming others, complaining about how life is not fair? Have you secretly, unaware perhaps, played the victim game? Decide today "No More" Decide today that I will no longer be a victim to my past, to anyone, or anything that is anti-progress. Decide today, I am 100% responsible for where I am in life right now, therefore I am free to begin to live the life I was created to live. That morning I made the decision to take 100% responsibility for my life. I no longer allowed my self-defeating thoughts to sabotage my dreams. I took full responsibility for my failures, as well as my successes. That morning I was free to live my dreams. It is important for you to understand that not taking 100% responsibility for your life keeps you a prisoner to your past whether you are aware of it or not. Think of your past as a "person". That person that takes pleasure in using the rope of life, tied around your neck, in the attempt to keep you from moving forward while suffocating you in the process. I went through a very emotional divorce and every time I endeavored to move forward my past was there to keep me from moving forward. There were times when I thought I had moved on, and then my thoughts would relive my past, causing me to have a panic attack. Causing me to remain in my past where I was beginning to feel comfortable in my sea of regrets. Your past is only happy when it can use fear to keep you from striving. But the day you decide to take 100% responsibly for your life your past has no other choice but to let you go. Taking 100% responsibility says I am now prepared, and ready to be changed. Jim Rohn said, "You must take personal responsibility. You cannot change the circumstances, the seasons, or the wind, but you can change yourself." You can change today if you decide right now to take 100% responsibility for your life right now. You can decide today I will become the person I am destined to be so that if my past comes looking for me again the new me will not respond. The one of many reasons why one may go back to being enslaved again by their past is because they attempt to break free without the thought of character development. You did not grow, and therefore that part of you which attracted your past makes it easy for you to go back when your past comes a calling. Make the decision today I will grow as a person. I will invest in myself. I will make personal development an important part of my life. I will declare that I will never again be a captive to my circumstance, or my past, I will not blame my circumstance for where I am in life now. I will take 100% responsibility for my past, as well as my present, and my future.

How do I know if I have not yet taken 100% responsibiltiy for my life?

Ask yourself these questions.

1. Do you constantly find yourself making excuses for your mistakes?
2. Do you find yourself a constant prisoner of the past?

3. Do you find yourself blaming others for your own problems?
4. Are you constantly looking to others to correct your life?
5. Are you misguided by thinking that "if only I could have this or that my life would be better off?"

I'm sure there are many more qualifying questions, but if you have answered yes to anyone of these questions then you are probably not taking 100% responsibility for your life. No need to be discouraged. The good news is that it is never too late for you to decide to take 100% responsibility for your life. As a matter of fact, it is as simple as saying today I decide today to take 100% for my life. Does that mean that overnight everything will fall into place? No! But overnight, just by deciding, you can begin the journey of healing, forgiving, living life to its fullest, and best of all freedom from our past circumstances. Will you make the decision today to take 100% responsibility for your life?

In the same realm, how do I know I have taken 100% responsibility for my life?

1. Do I take 100% responsibility for my mistakes without any explanation?
2. Have I acknowledged that I had a past without trying to cover it up?
3. Do I put the onus on me instead of putting the blame on others for my problems?
4. Am I looking at me instead of others in trying to correct my life?
5. Am I willing to be content with what I have, and believe that what I have now is the result of my taking 100%

responsibly for my life, therefore I do not need things to make my life better, it is already better?

Fleshing it out in Life's Application

You desire to start the process of building your building block to fulfill your dream by first taking 100% responsibility for your life, and you want to know how? Simply follow these Steps.

1. Find a quiet place where you know you cannot be disturbed. Make sure this time is scheduled so that you will not be bothered. This includes turning off your cell phone, and no electronic devices of any kind. You want to make sure there are no distractions.
2. Make sure you have a pen and a journal to write in.

3. You want to answer these four questions.
    a. What is holding me back from taking 100% responsibility?
    b. What parts of my life do I find myself not taking responsibility the most?
    c. How do I really feel about myself?
    d. How do I really see myself?
4. Get yourself an accountability partner. This is a person whom you consider to be a true friend. A person that knows you well. One who will tell you the truth even at the cost of your friendship. Ask your (AP) to be honest with you by asking them if they see you as your answers to the four questions above convey. Please

do not get upset. You are setting yourself up to beginning the journey of taking 100% responsibility for your life.

5. Make sure to speak positive affirmations in your life everyday by saying, "I am 100% responsible for my life therefore I am free to fulfill my dreams."

Answering these questions will help you see yourself as you really are. Life desires nothing more than to reward you, but it wants character building individuals. Individuals who do not make excuses of any kind for their misfortunes. By answering these questions truthfully, you will see yourself perhaps for the first time as you are. Please do not be discouraged by what you come to know to be true about yourself. It is in the swamp that the beautiful lilies often grow. Remember you want to be 100% honest with yourself. Taking control of your life requires 100% honesty from you. If you fail here, you will fail in taking 100% responsibility for your life. I look forward in continuing this journey with you in the next chapter. Let's go!

Building Block # 1
Decide what you want in life

"The first step in getting the things you want out of life is this: Decide what you want."

Ben Stein

If you could have been there with me that morning you would have seen me sitting on my bed staring up at the ceiling as the harsh reality that the end of the year will come, and as with many others, watching the year fly by with nothing significant to show for it. I realized that up until that point, as Paul Martinelli, President of the John Maxwell Company says, "Your beliefs drive your behavior." My negative thoughts had all these years pinned me up against the ropes even though outwardly I gave the appearance that I was this very positive person. My negative thoughts within, even though I had dreams, and aspiration, kept me in a stagnant position so that a whole year would pass by only to reflect at the end of the year feeling sorry for myself because I did not accomplish all I wanted to accomplish. My outward behavior, while I didn't realize it at the time was a reflection of my inward beliefs. At that moment, sitting on the bed, and talking to my wife I realize that I had to decide what I really wanted to do. I begin to take inventory of my life and asked myself the question what quality trait has been dominant in my life? It is amazing the answers one receives when the right questions are asked. As I looked at my life I discovered that the one quality trait that had been consistent in my life up until that point was encouraging people to be the best they can be. By nature, I am an encourager. That is something I know I can do with my eyes close. Before I could decide on what I wanted to do I needed to understand **first** what was I passionate about? Most people have a hard time deciding what they want in life simply because they haven't figured out what they are passionate about. I know that my passion is encouraging and inspiring people to accomplish their God-given dreams. Answering that question propelled me to make a decision that morning that I have not regretted it since. I have said to my audiences if you were to ask ten random people what they want to do in life perhaps two out of ten people would know the answer to that question. Just the other day I asked someone what is it that they wanted to do in life and they responded by saying, "I never thought about that". I believe most people fail in this area because they try and get what they want without first without knowing what they are passionate about. What most fail to see is that their passion forms the base for what they want in life not the other way around. Michael Jordan, a six-time NBA champion was passionate about winning. While most dream of winning a NBA championship most have not a winning passion. He allowed his passion of winning drive him to get what he wanted. It was that winner's passion that caused him not to give up when he was cut as a sophomore to return the following year and help his team win a championship. It was that passion that turned him into one of the greatest basketball players on earth if not the best. His passion gave him what he wanted. My passion in life is inspiring and encouraging people. It is this passion that is driving me to write this book. It is this passion that has taken me to Africa, the Philippines, the Dominican Republic, and parts of the states encouraging people. It is this passion that has led me to start my own business of inspiring others. It is this passion that has fueled my decision in deciding what I want. I remember it as it were yesterday. As I sat on my bed I said to my wife "I want to inspire people to fulfill their dream." I never thought that just by making a decision to live my passion that myriads of doors would open up. Today I am a certified John Maxwell Leadership, Trainer, and Coach, and a Les Brown Certified Speaker, and Trainer, A World

Class Champion Certified Speaker Trainer, and I am the C.E.O. of Above and Beyond X Factor LLC and a Jack Canfield Certified Trainer. None of these blessings would be my reality had I not decide to follow my passion. I am not bragging, or at least I hope not to come across as if I am. I am only stating to you that I have been able to accomplish these wonderful feet when I made a choice to add value to others. And if I can do this you can to. Are you missing out on your dreams because you have not yet decided what you want to do? I read a quote somewhere that said, "The first step in getting what you want out of life is to decide what you want." So, dear reader what is it that you want? You must start here if you are to fulfill your dreams. Napoleon Hill said, "Desire is the starting point of all achievement, not a hope, not a wish, but a keen pulsating desire which transcends everything". I recently read an article in the Forbes magazine that stated that 80% of American people are dissatisfied with their jobs. That means 80% of the American people go to a job they are not happy with. Can it be that you have 80% of people going to a job for convenience sake? Perhaps they're going to a job because they have bills to pay, or because they feel as if they have no other options. I call it working for a living for enslavement sake. Former NFL player Al Bubber Baker who played defensive end was fascinated with food. This was a long-standing passion of his. On his days off he would spend the day cooking. When the day came he finally retired he launched a barbecue restaurant and patented a way to debone spare ribs. He was so passionate about food that he convinced investor Daymond John to invest in his company in an episode of Shark Tank. Here is someone whose passion lead them to decide to open a restaurant. Again, I ask what is it that you want to do? Let your passion be the fuel that answers that question for you.

How can I decide what I want when I don't even know myself what I want?

1. **Start at a very simple place by asking this one simple question.** What am I passionate about? What can you do without even thinking about it that is so natural to you?
2. **What gives you satisfaction every time you accomplish something?**

3. What positive things has others said about me that is consistent with my passion?
4. What do I think about the most that is consistent with my passion?
5. What value would I enjoy doing for others even if it required no reward in return?

My intentions are not to belittle anyone's intelligence. I know this may sound simple, but it is often the simple things in life that are often the most profound. Confucius said, "Life is really simple, but we insist on making it complicated." Someone once said, "Simplicity is the key to brilliance." Do not try and complicate this. Your life's purpose and dreams are at stake. In deciding what you truly want today you are staking claim to your future. Embrace simplicity today and decide now what you want by discovering what it is you are passionate about. That morning I sat on my bed I knew that I wanted to help as many people as I can to fulfil their dreams. I'm passionate about inspiring people and encouraging people. I desire nothing more than to see the reality of the fulfilment come to existence in someone's life. If I can do that for one person reading this book I have accomplished my goal.

Fleshing it out in Life's Application

If you were asked what do you want to do would you be like most people not knowing the answer to that question? Have you a burning desire to accomplish great things, but do not really know where to start? Here are some steps you can follow.

1. What two quality traits do you find are dominant in your life? (**Example, Inspire and Encouragement**)
2. What do you think about most of the time that makes you happy every time you are doing that very thing?
3. What dreams have been locked up inside of you for a long time that every time you think about it tears start flowing down your eyes?
4. Is this passion of yours "other people" centered, or "you centered"?
5. Have you decided to pursue that passion?

Pondering on these questions will help you to draw out your passion in life. You will be able to unlock, what my friend Les Brown has coined, "the greatness within you" and live the life you were destined to live. You will be on your way of living the life you were created to live. Before moving on to the next chapter please take the time to apply the steps to your life. You have often heard it said that "knowledge is power", but I love what motivational speaker Eric Thomas has said, "knowledge alone is not power, applied knowledge is power." Knowledge is only power if it is applied. So, before you move on make sure that the information learned so far is applied.

Building Block # 2
Decide what price you are willing to pay

Nature cannot be tricked or cheated. She will give up to you the object of your struggles only after you have paid her price.
--- Napoleon Hill

When I was contemplating writing this chapter this thought came to my mind. ***If the price your willing to pay for the fulfilment of your dreams does not require a sacrifice from you that is painful then your dream is not worth the pursuit.*** As you are reflecting on the previous two chapters you should now have a clear understanding of what you are passionate about. But the real question you should be asking yourself is am I willing to pay the price that it will take to fulfill my dreams.

For you that price might be different. You see we don't all have the same dreams. The price comes in the sacrifices you are willing to make to achieve your dreams. I'm referring to a sacrifice that requires you to give up something so dear to you in order to fulfil your dreams. That sacrifice might be the pain of given up sleep, or it might be the pain of sleeping in late. It could also be the pain of watching too much T.V., or the pain of procrastination, or the pain of choosing leisure, instead of hard work. Whatever your pain may be your dreams must be worth the sacrifice. After deciding that I wanted to help people I had to find time and really decide what price I was willing to pay to succeed. In the last chapter, you heard me talk about my accolades, but if you could have known me before you would have known a person that was a master procrastinator, a person who made subtitle excuses, and a person who on the outside appeared to have it all together, but on the inside, I was really struggling. It felt as if life had me by the throat getting ready to hang me, and I had no control over it. A life of disorder, excuses for the lack of order, the procrastination, and myriads of other bad habits was finally taking its toll on me, and I was tired. You see my price was looking at all my deficiencies and asking myself was my dream of influencing people worth the pain I would experience of overcoming my debilitating habits. These things that often is the cause of us failing can sometimes become a source of pleasurable fantasy for us in becoming our safe comfort zone. It is that place we often go to when we are confronted by our dreams to come out of our comfort zone. I had wanted to write a book for years, but then the excuses came, "You failed English so many times in school." "You are not that bright." I even had a professor tell me to my face one time that "I was not a rocket scientist." These negative thoughts came rushing in my mind to keep me hostage to failure. Instead of writing the book I would go to my cubby hole of safety, and peace while at the same time strengthening the habit of procrastination, and many other bad habits that came along for the ride. The truth is my bad hits did not really bring me security. That was my mind deceiving me into thinking that so I would feel comfortable in my place of stagnation. The real truth is that my bad habits was really causing me pain. The pain of not writing that book. What if I did succeed? What if my book became a hit? You see the pain of not doing something to follow after your dreams is much more damaging and painful than pursuing your dreams. Think about it. A successful life may mean financial security for you and your family. A successful life may mean living life on your terms to pursue your goals and dreams. A successful life may mean the ability to be your own boss. Now imagine the pain of just the opposite. Your life dictated by everyone else except yourself. Your life encumbered by debt. Living from paycheck to paycheck, or as some have put it, "just over broke". A life where you are not your own boss, where everyone else but you is running your life. Imagine the stress on you and your family because of the false narrative you have placed on your pain. Your dream is worth the pain. I had to decide that day that I am willing to pay the price at any cost, no matter how painful it may be to fulfill my dream. I had to decide to step out of my comfort zone and embrace success while rejecting procrastination, and an undisciplined life. It was painful. Truth be told I am still battling it every day, but I am determined with the help of God I will succeed. I had an experience taught by my two-year-old daughter that taught me a valuable lesson regarding success. My daughter, when she was two had a fetish with our doorbell. Every time we had gone out and returned home she with her little brown eyes just had to ring the doorbell. One day I was driving home alone with my daughter Sarah on a hot beautiful day a thought came to my mind why not tell my daughter I have a popsicle for her in the icebox. As soon as I told her about the popsicle she began salving at the mouth. When I pulled up in the driveway, I turned the engine off, got out the car and unbuckled my daughter out of her seatbelt, took her out of the car, and put her down on the pavement. She ran to the door and for the first time in months my daughter didn't even notice the doorbell. I open the door, she runs through the living room unto the kitchen, makes a left to where the refrigerator is on the left. When I caught up to her she is standing there pointing up to the icebox saying, "popsicle". I opened the freezer box pull out a popsicle and hand it to her to her delight. That day my daughter taught me a valuable lesson. **When the**

picture of what you really want is greater than what you have always been doing then you will be successful. *Your mental picture must be greater than your pain.* Is the picture of your dreams stronger than the pain of giving up procrastination? Is your picture of your dream stronger than the pain of watching too much T.V., or leisure? When the picture of what we want is greater than our pain then success will come. That day I made a decision of inspiring others my picture became stronger than my debilitating habits. Again, I am still a work in progress, but I am moving towards my dreams. I'm writing this book to inspire you because my dream of doing so is greater than putting it off another day. The thought of inspiring you and knowing that your life is being transformed by the four solid building blocks is worth more to me than procrastination. What price are you willing to pay? Brian Tracy says, *"There is an interesting point about the price of success: It must always be paid in full-and in advance. Everyone wants to be successful. Everyone wants to be healthy, happy, thin, and rich. But most people are not willing to pay the price."*

Is your dream stronger than the price of sacrifice? Former President Barak Obama once said, *"If you aren't willing to pay the price for your values, then you should ask yourselves whether you believe in them at all."* I believe you are willing to pay the price or you would not be reading this book. I believe that you are committed to make the sacrifice of pursuing your dreams because your desire of making a difference is stronger than the price your willing to pay.

How do I know if I'm paying the price for my dreams?

Paying the price for my dreams requires that I know the sacrifices I need to make in order to achieve my dreams. Most people who would agree that paying the price is essential to fulfilling your dreams have no idea what price they have to pay. How do I know what price to pay if I don't know what I need to sacrifice? Here are some suggestions I recommend,

1. **Find a nice quiet place without distractions and take inventory of your life**. Ask yourself what is standing in my way of achieving my dreams. I find out that many of the things that stands in our way from

being successful are not bad things, but good things that I call non-essential.

2. **Is your life in motion or are you in a stop traffic condition?** If you answered yes maybe you need to hit the detour button to reset not your dream, but your path to your dreams

3. **Is there pain attached to the sacrifices you make to achieve your dreams?** Paying the price without the pain of sacrifice is only a setup to remain in our comfortable position of stagnation.

Someone once said, *"Every success has a measure of sacrifice; if you are not willing to pay the price, don't expect to get the prize"*. Are you willing to pay the price? Are you willing to make the necessary sacrifices no matter what it requires you to give up? Are you willing not to be like most people whose desire to be successful is not as strong as their willingness to pay the price? If your answer is yes let us flesh it out together.

Fleshing it out in Life's Application

How can you know that you are willing to pay the price to follow your dreams? Here are some questions you can ask yourself as you think about your dreams.

1. Is my dream stronger than my bad habits?
2. Is the price stronger than my dreams?
3. List every obstacle that might get in the way of me accomplishing my dreams
4. List all your positive traits that will help you accomplish your dreams

5. Take some time every day and focus only on your positive traits.
6. Everyday take one of your negative traits, write it on a piece of paper, and throw in the garbage. Do this every day until you have done this for all of your negative traits. Make sure to focus on your positive traits.
7. For every one of your negative traits speak the reverse into your life every day. For example, if one of your negative trait is not being on time you will speak the reverse by saying, "I am always on time"

We are laying down the foundation in lay down the 4 building blocks to greatness. This next step is important because it is the step that will propel you into the realm of untold wealth, and greatness, Prosperity, and a life of significance. Let us get there together!

Building Block # 3
Decide on a plan of action to take

Your attitude determines your actions, and your actions determine your accomplishment."
— John C. Maxwell

Is action something you do or something you respond to because of opportunities received by deciding what we want in life? When I decided to inspire people to fulfill their passions other opportunities came knocking at the door. One day as I was perusing on Facebook I saw an advertisement to become a John Maxwell Certified Speaker, Trainer, and Coach. I have read John Maxwell's books before but never in my wildest imagination did I envision becoming part of something he was associated with. I often associate opportunities with buying a car. When you buy a red Toyota Camry you never recognize red Toyota Camrys. But the moment you decide to buy that red Toyota Camry suddenly it seems as if everyone has a red Toyota Camay. Now is it that red Toyota Camrys didn't exist before you purchased one? You answered correctly! They did exist! But now that you have one your mind becomes open the myriads of red Toyota Camrys out there. When the mind is focused on a decision made to pursue your dream opportunities that were there before appears. John Maxwell Certified Team did not appear because of anything I had done. The truth is "I" appeared when I decided to pursue my dream of inspiring others. The opportunities were always there for me, but it was not until I decided that I began to realize opportunities upon opportunities. Not long after I joined the Les Brown Maximum Achievement Team and became certified as a Speaker, Trainer, and Coach. Other opportunities came and I am a World Class Champion Certified Speaker, and Trainer, and a Jack Canfield "Train the Trainer" Certified Trainer. Wow! I tell you this not to brag, but to make you aware that opportunities are there awaiting your decision to pursue your passion. I love this quote by Les Brown, "*Draw your line in the sand. Make your decision now and start taking action to really live your dream. By not taking bold steps to live your dream, not only are you missing out on fully living, but the world is missing out on the greatness you have to offer. Be bold!*" Decide today that you are going to unlock the greatness the world longs to see unleashed in you. You might be saying to yourself, "You make this seem as if it is so simple. If it is that simple why aren't more people successful?" I think the answer really is simple. You may not agree with me, but I really think that more people are not successful because they do not know what they want to do. You cannot put a plan of action together for something you don't know what you want. Chuck Palahniuk says, *"If you don't know what you want, you end up with a lot you don't."* Action is the response of knowing what you want to do. I heard a story about a minister who called his parishioner up to the altar to pray. While they were coming up the minister went up to one of his members and asked what are you praying for? The member replied, "nothing specific!" The minister answered by saying, "That is exactly what you are going to get, nothing specific." Your mind works best when a decision is made. As far as she could remember Julie Marie Carrier, also known as Julie Laipply, loved animals. When she was a little girl she would always tend to them in a way that made others believe she had a special connection with them. Those who knew her, and her passion for animals would suggest to her over and over, "you should be a veterinarian". As far as she could remember the suggestion of being a veterinarian was a theme song by those who loved her and thought she should work with animals because of her love for animals. Guess what she did? When she enrolled at Ohio State University she declared her major to be a Veterinarian. During her senior year she decided that she was going to participate in an exchange program overseas in France. One day, as Julie describes it, she was sitting down on a chair, staring at an opening window with a blank stare, facing the reality that her life up to this point has been a life fulfilling the dream everyone had of her. To one day be a Veterinarian. Julie at that point realized what many come to realize, that she was miserable living the life of the expectations of others, even if that expectation is sincere. Did she go off into the loneness of despair? No! Julie began to ask herself this question. What do I like to do that I have a good time doing it, and I would do it for free, but wouldn't mind getting paid for it? It was at this time Julie thought about spending summer months teaching youth's leadership principles. This was when Julie was most alive and had the most fun. It was at this point in her life Julie made a decision to pursue her passion of teaching youth's principles of leadership. Julie immediately changed her major and took classes now related to her purpose. Julie began to make plans and decisions entwined with her purpose. Julie contacted the University of Ohio State and convinced them to create a whole program teaching leadership principle and they agreed. What is the point to all of this?

Knowing what you want to do and deciding to do it is the fuel that ignites action. When Julie decided to teach leadership principles to the youth following her passion she immediately took to action. Since discovering your passion in life what actions have you taken to ensure that your passion will stay alive? Dalai Lama said, *"In order to carry a positive action we must develop here a positive vision"*. Julie had a vision. She knew what she wanted to do, and that ignited her to take action. Julie's plan of action kept her single minded, and on course. Sometimes, the lack of focus, we exhibit. is due to the fact we have not decided what we want to do. On that life transforming moment when I decided I wanted to help people to discover their passion in life I immediately put a plan of action together to do just that. My business was formed, I got certified with John Maxell, Les Brown, Brian Tracy, Craig Valentine, and Jack Canfield. There is no limit to where you can go and how many people you can help just by deciding what you want to do and taking action to accomplish it. Ask yourself this question how many people are still in the valley of despair waiting for you to take action on your dreams? I am 100% convince that had I not taken action I would not have had the opportunity to meet and connect with some amazing people. My friend and mentor Craig Valentine says, "*Most people look at the cost of doing something more than the cost of doing nothing.*" Could it be that the cost of doing something has cost many out of a life of happiness, and fulfilment. Sometimes we look at the price we have to pay to achieve our dreams and become discourage into doing nothing. I know someone who has an amazing dream, a great passion to want to achieve that dream, but their focus on the price they have to pay has caused them to put that dream on their shelve of life. I heard my friend and mentor Les Brown say, *"Many people die at 25 waiting to be buried at 65"*. I want you to ponder on this do you fall into this category, fall into this class because the cost of doing something was greater than your dreams? The fuel that ignites our passion is action. Put in another way Action is the fuel that keeps the passion going. One must be very careful to always remember that the starting point is always a strong passion burning deep within that drives one to take action. The mistake that many makes is to start off running before they know where they are running. Dr. Julie Connor, author of the book Dreams to Action Trailblazers Guide says *"Passion fuels dreams. Commitment fuels action. Get clear about what you want to do and why you want to do it. Take action. Your time is now."* Your passion says, "your time is now". So, take action.

How can I know if I am taking actions towards fulfilling my dreams?

Just knowing what you want to do and deciding the price you want to pay to achieve it alone will not in the long run help you to fulfill your dreams. There can be no break in the chain. All steps must be realized if you are to achieve your dreams or goals or else what you have is a beautiful, extravagant wish list. Arnold Glasow, a businessman, once said, *"An idea not coupled with action will never get any bigger than the brain cell it occupied"*.

So, what are the guidelines along the measuring stick of success that

determines where the point of the arrow is pointing?

1. Am I seeing progress made in reaching my goals
2. Is there excitement of victory and progress on my way to accomplishing my dreams
3. Do others see changes in the way I live my life that they did not see before
4. Is my vision becoming clearer and clearer?
5. Are others inspired by the actions I'm taking to fulfill my dreams

If you answered yes to every one of these questions, then you are probably moving to action every day. You can see your dream in front of you and it is driving you to reach it every sing day. Your every thought, and action spells of success, and you are compelled by a higher power to achieve your goal with assiduous, relentless pursuit.

Fleshing it out in Life's Application

Stephen C. Hogan, Social Entrepreneur, and Motivational Speakers says, *"You can't have a million dollars with a minimum-wage work ethic."* Most people have big dreams, but their work ethics do not match the level of their dreams. Antoine de Saint-Exupéry, a French writer, poet, aristocrat, journalist, and pioneering aviator says, *"A goal without a plan is only a wish."* How can you be sure that you are not daydreaming, and that you are living in the reality of action? Here are five key suggestion to follow that will help you along your journey to success.

1. What are the little indicators that you can see that are moving you towards your passion?
2. Connect with an Accountability Partner on an agreed time once a week to determine if your little indicators are moving everyday towards fulfilling your dreams or towards accomplishing nothing.
3. Commit yourself to those little action steps you are doing every day to bring you a little closer to your dream?
4. What are you feeding your mind?
5. Commit! Commit! and Commit to action every single day

Theodore Roosevelt once said, "Do what you can, with what you have, where you are". Are your ready to move to action on your dream?

Building Block # 4

Decide

The first step to getting the things you want out of life is this: Decide what you want.

Ben Stein

The last of the four building Blocks may seem simple in nature, but it is one of the hardest thing to get people to do. While it may appear simple getting people to make a decision is not as easy as one may think. It is for this reason I have this as the last building block, the foundation of the principles in this book. I want you to fix this thought in your mind. "To decide is to gain". Have you gain your dream? If you were there on that bright and sunny morning you would have seen an impatient father with his jubilant son who was running around a very crowded candy store. As the father stood at the front of the counter his son could be heard in the back of the candy room shouting, "which one should I choose?", "which one should I choose?". While the kid was running around the store trying to choose which candy he should choose the father shouts out to him, "Come on son, hurry up and choose, we don't have all day." As the son was running around among the myriads of candies he cried out, "These are my favorites" then pointing to another, "No these are my favorite. This the son did over and over as he went from aisle to aisle picking up one candy bar after another and then putting them back on the shelf. The little boy with all of the candies to choose from just could not make up his mind. The father who was standing up front watching all of this said in tones that reap frustration "Quick son, make up your mind, we have to go". Still the boy just could not make up his mind which candy he wanted so his father who by this time had just about enough walked to the back where his son had found himself, grabbed him by the hand, and walked out the crowed candy store empty handed. The young boy obviously now with tears in his eyes because he wanted them all but ended up with nothing because he couldn't choose one. What dream have you left behind because you couldn't make a decision? What dream have you left to stale on your shelf of life because of a lack of indecision on your part? How much of your life have you wasted because you have not yet decided to put these building blocks into practice? The time to make a decision is now. Katherine Hurst. who runs one of the world's largest law of attraction community says, *"If you are waiting for the right time that time is now"*. I would like to add if you are waiting for the right time to make a decision towards your dream that time is now. If you make a decision today to pursue your dreams your family, and friends will see you as one who is result oriented. You will accomplish more than the majority of this world's population implanting these building blocks. You will cut years off your life by not throwing your money away on meaningless theories and bribes that promises you riches without strategy and hard work. Finally, you will enjoy more time with your family, your life will seem to have more meaning as you do what you were called to do and help others along the way. You will enjoy the freedom of living a life not dictated by someone else's rule for your life. George Foreman in his book God in My Corner recounts an incident that almost cost him out of making a lot of money. His indecision at first almost cost him a whole lot of money. He says, "A business friend came to him with an offer". He said, "George, you've helped other companies by advertising their products. Have you ever thought about having your own product?" George said, "Later he sent me a small, slanted grill and asked me to try it out". George said, "I got busy with other things and forgot about it. A couple of months later, he called. "George, how do you like the grill?" "Oh, the grill. To be honest, I haven't tried it yet. Let me get back with you on that." After hanging up, I almost made one of the worst financial decisions I could ever make. I thought, *I really don't have time for this.* Fortunately, Mary changed my mind. "George, I've tried the grill and I like it a lot. The grease rolls right off and the food tastes really good." "Are you serious?" "Yeah," she replied. "I'll fix you a burger. "After taking a bite, I said, "Yeah, it is really good. And the grill is easy to clean up. I like this grill!" I wasn't thinking about making any money on the deal. I just signed the contract, so I could get sixteen free grills for my homes, friends, and family members. I never dreamed this opportunity would turn into a grilling empire! What if George had not decided to take that opportunity? We would never have heard of his grilling empire. Are we being robbed of your dream because you will not make a decision to begin the journey? How many people are waiting for you to add value to their lives by deciding on your dream? *What you waste time on others loose time on.* In other words, the more you procrastinate on saying yes to your dreams the more others are missing out on theirs. A car salesman said, 95% of the cars he sales are bought on impulse. People who often buys cars from him come to his dealership not knowing what kind of car they want to buy. This is how many treat their lives. They wake up every morning into life hoping something amazing will just fall right into their laps. What if you were to wake up every day knowing exactly what it is you wanted to catch? What if every morning getting out of bed for you was a joy and not a drag? Tony Robins, the motivational guru says, "*Your life changes the moment you make a new, congruent, and committed decision*". Are you ready for that life changing moment? Are you ready to begin to experience this life altering changing euphoria where life now has new meaning to you? Make up your mind right now that "now is the time".

The Purpose Decision Test

Circle the one that best describes you. One being the least likely. Five being the most likely.

1. I know exactly what my purpose in life is. 1 – 2 – 3 – 4 – 5

2. My everyday action aligns with my purpose in life. 1 – 2 – 3 – 4 – 5

3. When it comes to achieving my dream, I am focus 1 – 2 – 3 – 4 – 5

4. I wake up every morning excited about my day. 1 – 2 – 3 – 4 – 5

5. I allow others to fill my calendar. 1 – 2 – 3 – 4 – 5

6. My purpose is the result of what others said I should do. 1 – 2 – 3 – 4 – 5

7. I allow others to do my thinking for me. 1 – 2 – 3 – 4 – 5

8. I care what others think about me. 1 – 2 – 3 – 4 – 5

9. I'm really not clear what I want to do. 1 – 2 – 3 – 4 – 5

10. I am clear about my purpose. 1 – 2 – 3 – 4 – 5

11. My every day actions are aligning with my purpose 1 – 2 – 3 – 4 – 5

12. My dream is always kept before me. 1 – 2 – 3 – 4 – 5

40 – 44 says you are clear about your purpose in life, and your purpose is not controlled by the opinions of others.

35 – 39 says you are clear about your purpose, but you may not be sure how to go about it. Your purpose is not controlled by the opinions of others.

25 – 34 says you are somewhat clear about your purpose, and your life is somewhat dictated by the opinions of others.

24 or less says you are not clear about your purpose, and your life is dictated by the opinions of others. You might need the help of a Life Coach to help you

While this may not be an end – all to be all test it could serve as an indicator where you are right now in your life. The purpose of this test was just to give you an idea where you are in relations to your purpose in life.

Remember now is the time. The hour of excuses has passed, and you are now on the road acclaiming. Today is the day you say enough is enough and hello to your dreams. Decide right now I will choose what I want to do. Decide now I am willing to pay the price. Decide now I am willing to take action. If you decide now your life will from meaningless to meaningful. If you decide now you will attract others in your life that will help you along your journey, and that you will add value to along the way. If you decide now you will never again work a job for convenience sake, but rather you will now be working in your purpose. I have had the opportunity to coach many in seeing them live their purpose around the world. Nothing beats living the life you know you were called to live. **I AM YOUR FRIEND** and **I BELIEVE IN YOU.**

Author's Page

Jenks Brutus is an International Speaker, Trainer, and Coach. Jenks is a caring, transformational, inspiring, and encouraging individual who was born to serve others by adding value in helping others to fulfill their dreams. Jenks is certified in various professional training programs such as Train the Trainer by Jack Canfield, John Maxwell, Les Brown, and World Class Speaker by Craig Valentine. Jenks is also the author of the book 4 Building Blocks to Fulfilling Your Dreams.

Jenks's main area of focus is helping people create world class speeches through a process that will help them build the speech of their life. Jenks is also an expert in helping people in using their stories, and connecting with people to sell their products, motivate others, and create a life of purpose by sharing their story. Jenks is a leader who values people and seeks to lead by example. His leadership training will propel any individual, business, and or organization to pick up valuable tools that will move them to the next level.

Jenks works well with people and see others not as assets, but as partners along the journey to success. Working with Jenks He will make you feel special as if there is nothing you cannot accomplish. Jenks is the ultimate encourager, and this aspect of himself comes out in every presentation he delivers, whether speaking, training, or coaching.

If you're ready to go to the next level as a speaker, and you want to help others to excel in fulfilling their dreams then working with Jenks makes sense. Jenks along with his team, and mentors will help you in achieving your individual, business, or professional goals. Let me know how I can help you accomplish your goals.

Jenks Brutus

Leadership and Speaker Personal Development Trainer, and Coach

CEO of Above and Beyond XFactor LLC.

www.abxfactor.com

jenksb@abxfactor.com

www.ingramcontent.com/pod-product-compliance
Lightning Source LLC
Chambersburg PA
CBHW071415220526
45469CB00004B/1294